ONCE
IN THE
WORLD™

A JOURNEY IN HAIKU AND SENRYU

Terrance Brooks Boykin

Copyright © 2017 Terrance Brooks Boykin

All rights reserved. Published 2018.

ISBN-13:
978-0692865057

ISBN-10:
0692865055

Cover Photography: Terrance Brooks Boykin
Cover Image Technical Consultant: Thomas Barnes
Back Cover Photography : Earl Gibson III
Image: Southern view of the East River - New York, NY

IN MEMORY OF

Lorraine M. Boykin

ACKNOWLEDGMENTS

To my beloved friends and family who encouraged me to publish this collection of poetry.

WHAT IS HAIKU?

Haiku became popular as *tanka* poems in Japan during the 9th and 12th centuries. Initially, it was called *hokku* and writers such as; Basho, Buson and Issa were the first three masters of the haiku genre. The shorter version called haiku is an unrhymed, three-line poem with seventeen syllables. Although the practice of the five/seven/five syllable form is most popular, haiku poems are frequently composed with fewer syllable counts.

The art form of haiku emphasizes simplicity, intensity, and objective expression. As the form has evolved, many of the traditional rules have been transformed due to language, culture and new ways of experiencing the world. However, the philosophy of haiku has been preserved through focusing on a brief moment in time, a use of provocative and colorful images, and the ability to capture time, while revealing a sense of sudden enlightenment and illumination. This collection also includes the art form of senryu poetry. Senryu is the same as haiku poetry, with an emphasis on human nature and emotions, as opposed to the seasons or the natural world.

INTRODUCTION

We exist and thrive due to the hidden forces and graceful balance of the natural world. Nature's mystic energy influences how we choose to experience our lives from day to day and from moment to moment. What are the moments that have lead to you standing where you are right now in the world? It could have been a great achievement, a failure, a memory, or a random decision. Where will you go from here and when was the last time you gazed at the world around you with curiosity and the heart of immense appreciation for living?

Life is a series of endless and unique moments that will never come again. Along the way, we encounter sun rises and settings, textures and patterns, fragrances and sounds that unfold in conspicuous and inconspicuous ways.

When was the last time you opened your eyes to the nuances of the natural world's grandeur? How long has it been since you marveled at the intelligible fluctuations, seasonal transformations, and untamed migrations? How often do you take time to wander the sacred spaces of the forests, the deserts, the mountains and shorelines, while observing their contemplative complexities? When was last time you admired the impulsive uniformity of rural settings, and the chaotic harmony of modern cities?

The endless realms of the natural world continue to shape and influence the interconnections between all forms of life. As human beings, we all appreciate nature's delicate balance, and when the environment becomes unbalanced, we experience the undeniable shifts throughout the world. Looking at human beings and nature as independent forces is a tragic perspective that fails to open the doors that allow us to create and sustain an existence filled with valuable and authentic meaning.

Once in the World

Once in the World is a collection of poems that began with a commitment to write one haiku a day for one year. The intention of the journey was to expand my personal world view and to venture into spaces, new and familiar, with the hope of forging a fresh inner-resolve, while deepening my sense of appreciation within the moments of lived-experiences that emerged along my path. After one year, I had written over three hundred haiku poems. The haiku and senryu poems in this collection reflect observations and experiences that link human lives to the natural world in ways that will never emerge in the same way again. These insightful moments capture the hectic pace of urban living and the beauty of rustic landscapes. Each poem is a narrative that reveals the random and the primordial unfolding in the foreground and background of everyday occurrences.

In the tradition of the 16th Century Japanese artists who traveled the countryside writing poems, this collection is a poetic diary of experiences and explorations of cities, towns, forests, deserts, spaces and places throughout the United States. Like paintings on a canvas or photographed images, haiku captures the authentic allure of existence in ways that allow us to witness the unfolding of time, while capturing human perceptions, emotions, and cultural rituals.

Terrance Brooks Boykin

Birth

Full moon vanishing,

water falling through sunlight;

I taste the morning.

Summer canoes

race over glass reflections,

splashing in faces.

Shallow winter sands,

waves rush between tiny toes

making her giggle.

Frozen winter lake,

red scarves swirling around coats

into pirouettes.

Walking crooked bridge,

Afro blowing in the wind;

holding father's hand.

On Christmas morning,

tearing open large boxes

before reading card.

Midnight breezes roam,

floating cotton curtain hems

away from windows.

Desert sky pouring

darkness around naked skin;

measuring the moon.

Summer afternoon,

empty swings on playground

squeak before bell rings.

Blossoming red bulbs

dangle pollen on green stems

for rare honey bees.

Grey steam levitates

above burning, black kettle

whistling for tea.

Playground in summer,

two children raising their fists,

sudden change of heart.

Crimson roses

on tattooed forearms

embracing.

Catching fireflies,

floating over neighbors' fence,

eyeballs peep through palms.

The six-o-clock train,

winds blow grandfather's hat

down wooden platform.

Sitting in stroller

licking chocolate ice cream;

sudden drops of rain.

Red summer tulips

stand across meadow

shaking in the wind.

Summer camp,

tree branches growing wet shirts

on top of green leaves.

Hot summer sidewalk

shooting water from hydrant,

ankles jump the curb.

Mother & daughter

standing together in sun

preparing bouquets.

Black & white photo

captures artificial glimpse

of first day of birth.

Riding ferris wheel,

heels dangle over night skies

before drifting down.

Humid afternoon,

children draw squares on concrete,

chalk outline remains.

Iron fence leaning

over rows of fresh orchids,

shoe print in garden.

Reflections of sky

hiding glass wall of buildings;

orange light pours down.

Moon shines

on shallow puddle,

revealing a penny.

Summer butterflies

hiding behind rows of corn

above running feet.

Summer flea market,

string slips through fingers,

balloon rises.

Summer evening

breezes cooling brick houses;

lady bug climbs knee.

Grandmother's apron

protects bushel of apples

before slicing core.

Rocking back and forth,

see-saw sways in drizzling rain,

children run inside.

Banana leaves fall,

floating over deep puddles

spinning on concrete.

Windy summer storm

hurling rain drops on windshields,

a street lamp flickers.

Wooden cobalt gates

guard swimming pool in summer,

puppy fetches ball.

Hooded faces march

through October leaves at dusk,

knocking door to door.

Glowing summer sun

sinking across steel & glass,

shadows shift below.

Autumn rain

bouncing on waves & sand,

kicking stones.

She told him your name,

bowing her head in prayer,

eyes lifted her smile.

Maturing

Neighborhood alleys

covered with graffiti,

clothes hanging in sun.

6 in the morning,

bacon & coffee burnin'

coins roll of counter.

Hot plate of catfish,

folding napkins under chin,

too much tabasco!

A street musician,

sweating under summer moon

for pockets of change.

Spreading out blankets

over tall grass in shade,

ants march anyway!

French lilies waiting

in round baskets at market

for perfect stranger.

Thorns of pale roses

prick fingers of young bridesmaid

marching down the aisle.

He closes his eyes

beating, swirling pinata

for showers of sweets.

Wet cobble stone road,

6 inch pumps clicking, again

seconds after dawn.

Motionless full moon

quietly shifting the tides

of our emotions.

Sitting on porch steps,

doors slowly close behind him;

    crying in the rain.

Afternoon paper

rests on his knees over shoes;

    staring toward window.

Summer highway sun

baking leather seats,

lip singing to song!

1 Tuesday morning,

steam rises over coffee

before knock at door!

Embracing flowers,

invisible emotion

rises to her chest.

Sitting in the dark,

hearing voices from stages,

harmony fills room.

Big windy city

towers over the river

controlling the flow.

Summer evening,

fragrance of tulips drifting

table to table.

Drops of rain sliding

down chrome reflections of sky

on hot hood of car.

A glowing lamp post

over barrel of fire

dimming before dawn.

Quiet winter night,

cold fingers holding warm hands

in front of fire.

New Orleans winter,

dancing through narrow quarters,

beads fall from window.

Bending in the sun,

gathering a fresh bouquet

to hide behind back.

Dance under night skies,

mascara & eyeliner

stain new shirt & tie!

Jasmine aroma

mingle with tea-light candles,

flames flicker in glass.

Endless summer field,

big lips & curves in the grass;

fragrance becomes wind.

Hot dry wind

carries growl of car engine,

heart races in chest.

Fast evening train

blowing sound between buildings

rushing wind through hair.

Afternoon gossip

floating shop to shop

doorway to doorway.

Vase full of roses

standing near chocolate cake

still fresh from last night.

Wordless music soars

over Formica tables

before daylight comes.

Hands stroking her hair,

11 stems between teeth

under quarter moon.

Unfinished canvas

behind brushes in tin cans,

smell of turpentine.

Powerful night skies,

deepest blue behind moonlight,

black before sunlight.

Retracing footsteps

along snow covered sidewalk;

bump into strangers.

Winter evening,

sitting elbow to elbow

hearing spoken words.

Wisdom

Autumn afternoon,

leaves fall down from tree

tapping his shoulder.

Walking between trees,

tall & frozen under skies

discovering path.

Quiet winter wind

turns breath into clouds of smoke,

skates drift over ice.

Spring afternoon wind

blowing sleeves of leather coat,

he turns the corner.

A guitar player

on empty subway landing,

a dollar bill falls.

An old rusty pier

surrounded by blue ocean,

tai-chi in the rain.

Grey morning air stirs

uninterrupted silence,

branches snap on stone.

Guitar across knee,

roaming fingers inspire

familiar lyrics.

Magnificent tree

protects roof top, when thunder

answers lightening.

After spring harvest,

bushels fill the kitchen floor,

loud snap of string beans!

Slow running river

meanders through countryside

without shoes or feet.

Orange autumn leaf

dangling for another dance

with another breeze.

Hiking desert road,

footsteps crunching rocks & sand

between deep breaths.

7 graceful swans

swimming gently on water

hiding rushing feet.

Invisible web

between evergreen branches,

spider sleeps in silk.

Calm summer ocean

floating under jagged clouds,

water fills her ears.

In summer,

clay spins between wet fingers,

a shape emerges.

Purple umbrella

protecting hair from noon-sun,

sweat pours anyway!

Unfinished portrait

drying in the ocean breeze

watching strangers pass.

Saxophone player

drifting through open windows

while standing on ground.

Wild flowers in field,

he whispers secret to friend

then plucks a petal.

Growling lawn mower,

louder than the sound of crows

interrupting dreams.

Crowded subway train,

howling tunnel becomes night

before I can blink.

Neon signs flashing

under storm-laden clouds,

we buy and we sell.

Swaying knotted ropes

reach out to endless ocean,

rocking empty boats.

Sinking orange sun

changes places with the moon

in another sky.

Autumn melody,

the black & white ivory keys

gently strike the strings.

My father's, father

kneeling before eastern sun,

incense drifts through air.

The smell of damp soil

drying after summer rains,

a door swings open.

Sudden thunder storm,

burning candles on bookshelves

replace the darkness.

One winter morning,

a neighbor removes his hat,

smoke rises from skull!

Empty rocking chair

tips forward & backward

in evening wind.

Glowing sunset pours

over highway overpass

into rear windshields.

Crest of breaking waves

crashing over winter sands

leaving jagged stones.

A crowded cafe,

her smiling face tells the truth,

his trembling hands lie.

In summer traffic,

highway noises are replaced

with breath of Coltrane.

Wintry, tempest sea,

turbulence against smoothness,

black sky facing blue.

Walking in the rain,

the sound of thunder

interrupts a memory.

New World

Standing under trees

holding leaves that become birds,

skies become shadows.

Day after summer,

unbroken grey horizon

pushes breeze through sand.

Tall, juicy roses,

stems swaying around ankles;

taking one more step.

Hot winding asphalt

beneath black suits & white gloves,

sounding loud trombones.

Elderly woman

resting chin on folded hands,

she sips from her cup.

Sunday morning sun

shining on red fedora

over purple shoes.

Silhouettes create

shifting shadows in summer,

a balloon rises.

Fragments of laughter

echo around the fire,

you think you hear it.

December morning,

winter sleeps under dead leaves

around naked feet.

Vanishing full moon

floating and sinking brighter,

tightening embrace.

In sweltering heat,

rainbows reflect on asphalt,

eyes squint under brow.

Field of sunflowers

tilting in same direction

further than eyesight.

Winter afternoon,

freezes tall evergreen trees,

a branch trembles.

Moonlit reflections

bouncing light over river,

swimming over waves.

Moon over mountain

in western corner of sky

behind winding road.

American flag

over flowers & candles

blowing in silence.

Under turquoise sky

feathered headdresses swirling

in breezes of sage.

Morning coffee pours

over plates of eggs & toast,

strangers say hello.

Stars in the night sky

shining through open windows

of crowded kitchen.

Abandoned rose

stranded on rocks & wet sand,

petals float away.

Terrance Brooks Boykin

Fists digging in sand,

searching for walls of castles,

washed away by waves.

Swarming mosquitoes

surrounding river and sky

for taste of humans.

Summer evening,

a woman paints her eyebrows

darker than they are.

String of lights on trees

over footprints on sidewalk,

steam floats from sewer.

Just before midnight,

endless constellations glow,

a star shoots through sky!

Rising before dawn,

walking toward the shore

in sand without shoes.

Inside the window,

shoulder blades speak with black ink,

dripping sweat in sun.

Painted concrete road

frozen under colorless sky,

sun clearing the clouds.

.

Magnificent pier

reaching out to rising sun

across glass ocean.

Painted steel & stone

standing under crescent moon,

neon lights flicker.

Woke up this morning

in 7 feet of water,

unmade beds floating.

Dry, open desert

resting silently in sun

for hiking soles.

Long winterless road

basking in the brutal sun,

standing with brothers.

Endless winter sky

behind frozen mountain tops,

floating on lake.

Waves rushing away

bubbling into liquid clouds

beneath golden sun.

In autumn sun light,

braiding thick, woolly Afro

between mother's knees.

Shadows through windows

further than my voice's call,

shift in the distance.

River reflection

resembles old photograph,

why do mirrors lie?

Black wings stretching out

against dangerous blue sky

rising & rising…

www.ingramcontent.com/pod-product-compliance
Lightning Source LLC
Chambersburg PA
CBHW071203090426
42736CB00012B/2429